PETERSFIELD
Seen and Remembered

Des Farnham and Derek Dine

Hampshire County Library

ISBN 0 901406 05 8

Printed by Hampshire County Council Printing Works

Notes on the Authors

Derek Dine is Divisional Librarian of the Central Division of Hampshire County Library. He is a keen amateur photographer and took all the modern photographs for this book during 1981. He is also responsible for the modern photographs in companion volumes published by the County Library in 1978, 1979 and 1980 entitled 'Winchester Seen and Remembered', 'Havant Seen and Remembered' and 'Andover Seen and Remembered'.

Des Farnham is Senior Librarian at Petersfield Library, a position he has held since 1978. He has prior connections with East Hants being formerly Librarian at Liphook/Grayshott and Rural Services Librarian at Petersfield. Originally from Dorset County Library service he has a keen interest in local history and is a member of the Petersfield Area Historical Society.

Acknowledgements

The Authors wish to thank the following for permission to reproduce old photographs.
Petersfield Area Historical Society, Mr. David Allen,
Hampshire County Record Office, Mr. W. Geer, Mrs. B. M. Wardle,
Pamlyn Prints, Mrs. A. Sutton.

Thanks are also due to:
Geoff Salter (Deputy Divisional Librarian, S.E. Division), The Staff of Petersfield Library, The East Hants Post.

John Woodhead, Hampshire County Library Design and Display Officer, responsible for the layout and design of this publication.

Introduction

During the 12th Century William of Gloucester, wishing to increase his revenue from the Manor of Mapledurham, created the new town of Petersfield. At that time the manor was centred on the village of Buriton and Petersfield receives no mention in the Domesday Book. The town was sited on a sandy rise between two streams beside the new church of St. Peters in the Fields. It was planned with streets radiating from a centre near the present junction of the High Street and the A3. Plots of land, burgess plots, were leased to craftsmen and tradesmen at a peppercorn rent. The town flourished and by the middle of the century was one of only five towns to have a Guild Merchants.
Over the centuries the buildings changed but the boundaries mostly remained the same. Houses and shops were individually replaced or repaired and now provide an interesting mixture of construction and style, showing the changing fortunes of the town. Petersfield's prosperity was based on the cloth and leather industry and the town's position as a centre for the farming community. It was granted the status of a market town in 1373 and its prosperity fluctuated over the years until the decline of the trade in cloth and leather in the 17th Century.

Petersfield's later importance was based on its position astride the communications route between London and Portsmouth. The coaching trade provided the impetus for expansion along the London Road and the growth of the coaching inns — the White Hart and later Red Lion, Green Dragon and Dolphin. The completion of the London — Portsmouth railway and the station at Petersfield in the mid 19th Century gave a boost to the west of the town and resulted in the building programme which included Chapel Street and Lavant Street.

The population of the town at the beginning of the 19th Century was under 1,500. The town returned two Members of Parliament until the Reform Act and in 1822 the number of voters was about 150.

Statue of William the Third

Sir William Jolliffe, MP for the borough of Petersfield from 1734—1741 left £500 on his death to buy a statue of William of Orange. The statue was cast by John Cheere and was erected in the courtyard of Petersfield House. The house was demolished in 1793 and the statue, originally brightly gilded, was moved to the square in 1812 . It decayed visibly over the next century and in 1911 was bought by the Urban District Council. Money was raised by public subscription and the statue restored and partly remodelled with recut inscription on a resurfaced pedestal. The restored statue was unveiled in 1913 and has remained in its central position apart from a brief overhaul in 1963.

Behind the statue can be seen the new library opened in June 1981. Beside it the attractive Victorian exterior of 'The George' masks a much older building, once part of a much larger inn. In the early 19th century the inn was divided into three as the increased importance of the London Road caused a decline in trade. The library occupies the site of the Coffee House Tavern—a temperance establishment offering hot and cold baths for over fifty years until the 1920s when it became the Southdown bus office, Mrs. Moulder's Card Shop and for a short time the Brunswick Laundry. The site on the corner of Sheep Street was once Mr. Shepherd's saddlers shop but most will remember it as Money's furniture and antique store. These buildings were demolished in the 1960s to await the eventual construction of the library.

Castle House — The Square

This magnificent ivy covered Tudor House was demolished in 1913 to make way for the present Post Office and Midland Bank. Castle House was built in the late 16th Century and has been the residence, over the years, of many influential people including John Jolliffe and John Bonham Carter, MP. The building was the chief architectural feature of The Square and at one time the gardens were extensive. The Post Office was opened in 1922.

The Square
Number 1 The Square, now the Donkey Cart, is one of the oldest
buildings in the town and was once a farmhouse. At the time of the older
photograph, Number 1 The Square was the grocery and china shop of
Henry May, later to become George Bailey, greengrocer and seed
merchant. Number 5 The Square, Lloyds Bank, was built in 1800 and sold
in 1911 to the Capital and Counties Bank as occupiers. The Square
Brewery has been the site of beer retailing for many years. The building
with the sun blinds was the premises of Thomas Privett, silk mercer,
costumier and outfitter, later to become a similar business run by Norman
Burton.

11

Cattle Market 1904

Petersfield has always been a prosperous agricultural community. The rights of the manor and borough of Petersfield were granted in 1599 by Elizabeth I and included the markets, tolls and other advantages. These rights were purchased by the Urban District Council in 1911. The cattle market was a meeting place for farmers from the surrounding area. Sheep and pigs were kept in pens in the centre and cattle tethered to the railings. Prior to the 18th century the butchers stalls, or shambles, were in rows across the northern half of The Square, which was not completely paved until 1902 to comply with Ministry of Agricultural regulations. The animals finally gave way to cars and the last cattle market was held in 1962.

Cattle Market

The buildings in the two photographs are remarkably unchanged. The only new building is the Co-operative Stores. The first on the left in the old photograph is that of W. T. Neighbour—grocer, baker and wine merchant, later to become Forest Stores. The building was rebuilt for Fine Fare retaining the original first floor facade. The Corn Exchange was built in 1866, the ground floor being an open hall which could be segregated into stalls for corn trading. This building was also the only one in the town large enough to be used as a concert hall and is probably better remembered as such. Now an estate agents, the lower half of the building has been altered considerably while the upper facade is relatively unchanged.

The Square—East Side 1897
The older photograph was taken during Queen Victoria's Diamond Jubilee celebrations in 1897. The Golden Horse public house on the left was originally the Bakers Arms but changed when the gilded statue of William III was moved to the Square in 1812. The Golden Horse was demolished at the beginning of the century to make way for the Co-operative stores which was in turn demolished along with the building occupied by Claytons, later Shepherds, the Saddlers. This in turn was replaced by the present Co-operative building. Manchester House occupied by Gammon Brothers in the photograph was soon to become Rowland Son & Vincent, drapers and house furnishers.

St. Peters Road

New Way was renamed St. Peters Road in 1894. It was originally cut by John Jolliffe as an approach to Petersfield House, which was commenced in 1731 on the site now occupied by the Police Station and Infants School. The house was demolished in 1793 and the statue of William Third, which originally stood in a circus outside the house, was moved to the Square in 1812. The gardens of Petersfield House stretched south west to beyond the stream which was once an ornamental canal. The Police Station was erected in 1858 and the Infants School in 1894. The view in the photograph has changed little over the years as there has been a Bell Inn on the corner site since at least 1821.

Dragon Street C1905

The Green Dragon was once one of the best known coaching inns of Petersfield. Until the 18th Century the inn occupied the site on the opposite side of the street, now Dragon Antiques. The present Green Dragon began in the 18th Century but until 1976 it was known as the Sun Inn. The building has a Regency frontage but originated from the 16th Century and was timber framed.

The building next door, now the Toby Jug, has a late 16th Century frontage (and was originally a two bay, box framed timber structure with wattle and daub noggin and a central brick chimney). The building was enlarged in the 18th century and again a century later, probably forming two houses. This is followed next door by Dragon House, originally a 6th Century building now with an 18th Century facade. On the right of the picture is Moulds who have operated from this site since 1905.

Red Lion

With a frontage onto both College Street and Heath Road the Red Lion
has featured in the social and political progress of the town for many
years. The Tap Ale House in Heath Road was built in the late
16th Century. The site was gradually expanded and by the late 18th
Century the many buildings were known as the Red Lion. The large
buildings to the north is the brewery built by Lukers which burnt down in
1933, the remains being used for a time as an off licence. The Antrobus
Almshouse, built in 1624 for the relief of poor men and women, and
demolished in the 19th Century, lay to the north. This part of the A3 is the
narrowest part between London and Portsmouth.

19

High Street North C1925

In the early 19th Century Winton House was converted to a private house. It was used as a surgery, then in 1921 it became a women's club and in 1948 the County Library took over the ground floor. At the same time Winsers was converted into a shop where recent repairs have unearthed an Elizabethan fireplace dated circa 1590.

The first shop on the left in the old photograph is that of Henry Gander, butcher and fishmonger and the premises next door housed Childs bookshop and printers. Both establishments were part of the commercial life of the High Street for many years before being demolished to make way for a supermarket.

High Street North

The most important building on this side of the High Street is Winton House. Originally Winton House and Winsers formed part of the White Hart Inn, Petersfield's foremost coaching inn until the 18th Century when the Dolphin took over. The original inn had extensive lands including part of the area now taken up by the car park. Recent building behind Winton House unearthed the site of a bowling green, which throws new light on the story that Samuel Pepys once played bowls while staying in the town. At one time Winton House was joined to Winsers by a gateroom forming an entrance to the yard. There was a private way through the yard to College Street with a convenient entry for London traffic near the present White Hart, a route recently re-opened as a footpath to the car park and Folly Market.

21

High Street South

The Dolphin Hotel was built in the 18th Century and replaced an older building which had been divided into several tenements. With frontages onto both Dragon Street and the High Street the hotel was in a good position to exploit the growing coach trade between London and Portsmouth. The building was extended over the years and the accommodation and stables covered a large area. William Cobbett was an appreciative guest in 1825 when the Dolphin was one of the foremost coaching inns in Petersfield.

During the 1914-18 war the building was used as a Red Cross Centre and in 1919 became the County High School for girls. It was demolished in 1965 after being vacant for some years. The present scene of flats and shops was erected in 1966 and won a National Trust award for civic design.

The Victorian Post Office next to the Dolphin was built in 1892; previously the service was operated from the stationers and newsagent shop on the opposite side of the High Street. The next house has an attractive Regency frontage hiding a much older structure — it may be remembered as the dental surgery of Mr. Charles Dickens. Both buildings were demolished at the same time as the Dolphin. The War Memorial was paid for out of public subscription to commemorate the 1914-18 war; after the Second World War the Urban District Council added a second commemorative tablet. Unlike many old market towns Petersfield has always been blessed with a wide High Street and many of the kerb stones are regarded as the originals.

Punch and Judy—High Street

The early 17th Century house on the south side of the High Street is dated 1613 although the doorhead and windows are later additions. The house is Tudor framed and each storey slightly overhangs the other. The doorways are attractive but the conversion to a shop obscures the original building, In 1911 the premises were used for a veterinary surgery; since then it has become popular as a tea room and adjoining shop.

St. Peters Church—The Square

The church appears to have been built in the early 12th Century and was known as St. Peters in the Fields. Originally a cruciform building, it consisted of nave, chancel, north and south transepts and possibly a central lantern tower. Until 1886 St. Peters was a chapelry of Buriton and although enlarged in the 12th Century only the east wall of the central tower remained by the 18th Century. In 1873 the church was restored and given a sacristy, organ chamber, new Norman east windows and clerestory. The parish registers date from 1558 and the last burial took place in 1856.

Town Hall—The Square

This print shows the buildings that were originally in front of St. Peters Church. The first building on the left, adjoining the Market Inn, was the Town Hall built in 1828 on the site of the old market hall. Similar in design it had a meeting room above an open arched hall where farmers traded and the town cells at the rear. You may recognise the stone arches and parapet copings incorporated in the gentlemen's convenience—originally built as a store for market furniture. The next building was the Hampshire Post Offices linked to the Town Hall by a first floor room forming an arch through which churchgoers passed. The Queen Anne house next door was known as the Old House and used as an auctioneer's rooms, while the three storied building, now a solicitor's office, was well known as the Commercial Hotel.

Petersfield, Sheep Street.

Sheep Street

There are a number of possible derivations for the name of the town's quaintest street. It could be from the Ship Inn which once stood near the site of the present Royal Oak. In 1653 the street housed a slaughterhouse and wool warehouse; as the lower end of the street was the centre of the trade in fleeces this could have given the street its name. It could also have come from Cheap Street as it led away from the market. During recent building, finds of roof tiles, glass, metal, bones, flint and oyster shells indicate continuous occupation of the area since the 13th Century. The street has some fine examples of 16th and 17th Century buildings with the original timber frontages in place and some older buildings have 18th Century frontages. The right hand side of the street was mainly residential while the opposite side housed a few shops. Shirleys has been a shop for over a century and the fish and chip shop has a long history as a fishmongers.

31

The Spain—Goodyers

John Goodyer, one of the earliest English botanists, lived for many years in the large house on the left now named after him. The origins of Goodyers are mainly Tudor but it is possible that it could have been two medieval houses brought together in Tudor times. It was referred to as the Great House in 1461. The front of the house, like many others in the town, has had an 18th Century facade added and has been sympathetically modernised leaving many features unspoilt such as the Tudor fireplaces. John Goodyer moved to the house during the 1620s just before his marriage and died there in 1664. A plaque stating "John Goodyer Botanist and Royalist (1592—1664) lived here" can be found on the house.

The house on the right, Tullys is the oldest house in Petersfield. It is believed to have dated from the 14th Century and was a halled house—one large room from the ground to the rafters with a platform forming a first floor and a hole in the roof for the smoke to escape. The older photograph shows the remains of a hipped roof and a jetted upper storey on a much wider building. A popular theory on the origins of The Spain is that it was here that Spanish merchants bought their cloth.

The Spain—Looking Towards the Hospital

At first glance these two photographs have little in common but the house on the right can be recognised by the buttresses on the pavement. This house has been extended over the years and the cottages next door demolished. The building on what is now the hospital car park was once Aylwin's sweet shop.

The Cottage Hospital was built "to establish a hospital at Petersfield for the acception and medical and surgical treatment of severe cases of disease and accident amongst the poor". The money for the building and running costs was raised by donation and annual subscriptions. The contract was given to Mr. Gammon and a site provided by Lord Hylton; the building was opened in 1871 at a cost of £480.

Charles Street C1914

The first building on the left, Spring Cottage, is dated 1882. Before the coming of the railway C1859 this would be a rural view of Gallows Field with the Drum River crossing it. Charles Street was part of the development in the 1880s, heralded by the building of the station, which included Lavant Street and Chapel Street. The street has always been predominantly residential except for Number 2 which has always been a shop. The GPO STD exchange was built in the 1960s and can just be seen on the right of the modern photograph. The street is now popular as a parking area for commuters using the station.

Railway Station

The direct line from London to Portsmouth came later than the lines to other south coast ports and was a poor relation until electrification in 1937. The final link between Godalming and Havant was constructed by the London and South Western Railway Company. It is interesting to note that both Petersfield and Godalming have virtually identical station buildings. This reflects the fact that they were once the only stations on the final link and were given equal status. The importance of Petersfield for railway operations increased in 1864 when the Petersfield Railway Company opened the branch line to Midhurst. This branch line closed in 1955 before the Beeching era and the goods yard was shut in 1969. The Railway Hotel was built, as it name suggests, to solicit trade generated by the railway. In 1900 it offered a special tariff for cyclists and commercial travellers. Around 1910 a ''mad sailor'' went berserk in the town with a rifle and finally shot a woman in the yard of the Railway Hotel.

LONDON & SOUTH WESTERN RAILWAY.

On Thursday, 23rd July,

SPECIAL CHEAP DAY EXCURSION

TO

LONDON

(WATERLOO STATION),

AS UNDER :—

		A.M.	
Midhurst	- depart	10.38	} 3/6
Elsted	- ,,	10.44	
Rogate	- ,,	10.49	
PETERSFIELD	,,	11.10	} 3/=
Liss -	- ,,	11.17	
Liphook	- ,,	11.29	

WATERLOO arr. about 12.50.

Return by any Ordinary Train.

CHAS. J. OWENS,

General Manager.

Lavant Street

Lavant Street is part of the development that followed the building of the railway. At the beginning of the century the street was mainly residential but gradually the elegant houses gave way to shops. The street now offers convenient parking and some of the shops have retained their atmosphere of the small family concern all too often absent nowadays. On the right the building now occupied by Napier Antiques was well known as A. J. Williams the chemist, followed by Binsteads grocer and butcher's shop and the Girls' School governed for many years by the Richardson sisters. The premises at the end of the street (now Menzies) was the drapers and milliners shop of Wells and Rush.

39

LAVANT St POST OFFICE.

LLEWELLYN E. BRADLEY.

Bookseller. Stationer. News Agent. Fancy Repository.

Lavant Street Post Office C1907

The photograph of Lavant Street Post Office was taken around 1907. The site, now K Shoes, was occupied for a short time by Llewellyn E. Bradley as a bookseller, stationer, newsagent and fancy repository before becoming a Post Office. Mr. Bradley moved across the road to Number 2, now occupied by Mellows, soon after the photograph was taken. The illustration is a good example of what must have been meant by the term 'fancy repository'.

London House C1923

Originally J. S. Roach, provisions dealer, London House was taken over by W. J. Fuller at the turn of the century. The business was well known to shoppers in the 1920s and 1930s, when the photograph was taken, as a grocers, bakers, provision merchants and tea and coffee specialist. In 1900 the speciality 1/8d. tea was advertised as "strong, pure and delicious. Blended with care and suits the water of the neighbourhood". Mr. Fuller was a pillar of the Congregational Church and a just man although he kept strict discipline in his shop. He employed about 25 staff all of whom were provided with aprons and overcoats. Facing into Chapel Street were the bakery and stores. Here tea, coffee, sugar and other commodities arrived in bulk and had to be weighed and packed into small quantities for sale. As can be seen by the modern photograph London House is now a subject of controversy.

Dukinfield Church Street

Chapel Street

Before 1860 this area was rural in outlook apart from the Drum and a few cottages. The name comes from St. Andrews Chapel which once stood opposite the north end of the present street. In 1740 it was called Ramsbridge Street after the Ramsbridge over the Drum River and in 1773 it was the main route from the Square and known as Winchester Road.

The view in the photographs which looks up the street towards London House show that it has always been a busy shopping area. The two men in white on the right of the older picture, outside what is now Bannisters are probably from Adams the butchers. The building now occupied by Nationwide was originally the Swan Inn, giving its name to Swan Street. It later became the site of the much loved Petersfield Electric Theatre.

International Stores C1930

The alleyway between International Stores and Wilkins now leads to the car park. A century ago D. E. Hobbs moved his blacksmith's business from Dragon Street to the site indicated in the old photograph. He operated his smithy, wheelwright and agricultural implement agency from here until the 1930s when he moved to Swan Street. Mr. Seward also ran a similar business from what is now the road leading to the car park. At the beginning of the century W. Seward was listed as engineer, millwright, brassfounder, steam roller and threshing machine proprietor and steam haulage contractor. One of his specialities was the repair of fairground roundabouts and organs.

The International Tea Company, later International Stores, have occupied the same site since the 1890s. Many people nostalgic for the prices and quality of the photograph of the shop front will also remember the bacon slicing machine clearly visible through the window.

47

Station Road

Methodism was introduced to Hampshire around 1750 and John Wesley visited Portsmouth over 20 times. By 1800 there was a Methodist group in Petersfield and in 1870 a chapel was opened in New Way; it is now St. Peters Hall. By 1901 the site for the church pictured above was bought and the church opened in 1903. The hall, vestry and kitchens were modernised and extended at a later date.

In 1903 the church was known as the Wesleyan Methodist Church and with the Methodist Union in 1933 the Primitive Methodist Chapel in Windsor Road joined with it but the Windsor Road Chapel remained independent for services until 1940.

College Street

The photograph shows the United Reform Church (formerly the Congregational Church) and the public hall in College Street. The church was opened in 1801 and in 1872 received its more familiar frontage.

The hall to the right of the church was built by the British and Foreign Bible School and was known as the British or 'Penny' School because of the fee. It later became the College Street Public Hall and some may remember it as a garage or coachworks. It was demolished about 1950.

Churchers College

Founded in 1722 by Richard Churcher, an East India Company merchant who left enough money to build and endow a school for 12 local boys who were to be taught English, Mathematics and Navigation and 'thereafter be apprenticed to the East India Company'. The Endowed School Act of 1876 and the gift of a ten acre site at Ramshill by William Nicholson, one of the governors, persuaded the Board to sell the old College in College Street and erect a new school at Ramshill. The school closed in June 1877 and reopened in the present Gothic style building in September 1881.

Sheet Mill 1910

Three mills are mentioned in the Domesday Book as being in this area.
The date on the mill is 1740, but this Mill and Sheet Bridge Mill are
believed to have been in existence in the 11th Century. They were
probably wooden structures on stone bases. The mill on the left in the old
photographs was still being worked in 1910 when the photographs were
taken. The horse and cart is being loaded with sacks of flour milled on
stones driven by the water wheel.

Sheet Mill

The mill was converted to a private dwelling in the 1930s. The four cottages facing the mill are also interesting. The left hand pair have been converted into one cottage and modernised without losing any character. During the renovation a date stone was found in a wall and reset in an outer wall. It reads "Built 1606 repaired 1867." During the last conversion in 1970 a number of French coins were found in a cellar and it is supposed that they may have been left by French prisoners of war who were possibly billeted in the cottage whilst working on the cutting through Butser Hill. The cottage may have been a bakery at one time.

Sheet Green

The Green has always been the centre of the village but it was not always on such a steep slope, as the main road was built up for safety. St. Mary's Church, in the parish of Petersfield, was built in 1869 from the design of Sir Arthur Blomfield. The chestnut tree was planted in 1897 to celebrate Queen Victoria's Diamond Jubilee. There is a story that the original tree, planted further down, was burnt by the lights hung around it to celebrate the occasion. The replacement was protected by iron stakes made by the local blacksmith.

Kettlebrook Cottages
These picturesque cottages near the Harrow at Steep look as if time has passed them by. The original thatch is still evident in the older picture. The cottages get their name from their position on Kettles Brook which runs in front of the cottages. The most likely origin of the name is from the Old English "citel" meaning deep valley.

Petersfield Fire Brigade 1910

Petersfield Voluntary Fire Brigade was formed by invitation of the Lighting Inspectors in 1889. The engine and equipment were kept in what is now the ladies toilet in St. Peter's Road. The horses were hired privately and the funds were raised by public subscription and grants from the Urban District Council.

62 In 1904 the original fire engine was replaced by a Shand Mason Steam Fire Engine. A fire used to be lit under the boiler producing the steam power to drive the pumps. At first it was pulled by horses but later it was towed by a lorry. Since the lorry travelled faster than the horses more draught was produced causing problems with the boiler. The picture shows the machine at work in East Meon. In 1924 Petersfield received its first motorised fire engine—a Dennis.

Bibliography

MINTY, E. Arden. Some Account of the History of Petersfield. Bodley Head 1923.

PETERSFIELD AND DISTRICT OFFICIAL GUIDE.

PETERSFIELD AREA HISTORICAL SOCIETY—PETERSFIELD PAPERS.

No. 1.   Petersfield Place Names.
No. 3.   The Inns of Petersfield.
No. 5.   Petersfield in Tudor Times by W. M. Whiteman.
No. 6.   Petersfield Under the Later Stuarts by E. M. Yates.

PETERSFIELD AREA HISTORICAL SOCIETY BULLETINS.

THE VICTORIA HISTORY OF THE COUNTIES OF
ENGLAND—HAMPSHIRE AND THE ISLE OF WIGHT.